Monetary Correction

A PROPOSAL FOR ESCALATOR CLAUSES
TO REDUCE THE COSTS OF ENDING INFLATION

MILTON FRIEDMAN

Nobel Laureate 1976
Professor of Economics,
University of Chicago, 1946-77

Published by
THE INSTITUTE OF ECONOMIC AFFAIRS
1974
THIRD IMPRESSION 1978

First published July 1974
Second Impression November 1974
Third Impression June 1978

by

THE INSTITUTE OF ECONOMIC AFFAIRS

Printed in Great Britain by Oyez Press Limited

Contents

[4]

Preface

IEA Occasional Papers are designed, inter alia, to present to students and teachers of economics, and to laymen interested in economic thinking, material originally delivered to or published for other groups of listeners or readers.

Occasional Paper 41 is by Professor Milton Friedman. He had agreed to write a *Paper* for the IEA on the economics of indexation or 'monetary correction'. The economies of scale in cerebral and literary production made it convenient for him to propose an amplified and revised version of an article he was writing for *Fortune*. The text has been anglicised in a few places for British readers and footnotes added on nearest British equivalents or parallels.

Professor Friedman suggested that a discussion of a 'tabular standard' by Alfred Marshall should be added. It shows that classical economic thinking was aware of the task of preventing economic relationships from being distorted or disrupted by inflation.

We have also added, especially for students and teachers, a short history of references to and discussion of the subject by British and other economists and a bibliography by Mr Brian Griffiths of the London School of Economics, and for all readers a Note on 'Fiscal Drag' and several Tables and Charts to show the British context of the debate: the recent acceleration of inflation in the British economy. Inflation may be world-wide, but since 1970 it has been twice as fast in the UK as in the USA and faster than in most other Western economies (Chart 4: Insert, p. iv).

As would be expected from the leading world exponent of monetary economics, Professor Friedman presents a scholarly (if here brief) analysis of inflation and a cogent case for making the only known effective cure—monetary restraint—politically feasible by a method—'monetary correction', indexing, indexation, escalator clauses (or threshold agreements) in contracts—that he says is not ideal but the only one in view that offers a hope of mitigating the side-effects of ending inflation. Inflation in Britain has accelerated since 1969 under Labour and Conservative governments to the point at which the tried method of incomes or prices policies and the untried cure of monetary self-control may have to be replaced or supplemented by unconventional methods.

The debate on 'monetary correction' is now yielding proposals for policy. Professor Friedman's analysis and advocacy has produced a Bill in the United States Senate. Readers in Britain, with its faster rate of inflation and unique institutional environment, might raise questions that seem especially stubborn here: whether the apparent effectiveness of monetary correction in Brazil, Canada, Israel and elsewhere would be reproduced in Britain, with its entrenched institution of trade union power which might permit upward indexing that served the interest of the hierarchy of officials or of the highly-organised rank-and-file, but veto relative downward, i.e. less rapid upward, indexing, as it has done other Labour and Conservative proposals it disliked; whether any measures to contain inflation would be supported by the public as long as it was encouraged to believe that government had to raise revenue for essential expanding activities, or that 'full employment' meant that no man had to change his job or move his home; whether indexing would inhibit a fall in real wages in declining industries that persuades labour to move to expanding industries; whether politicians who shrink from the reduced government expenditure, higher taxes or increased borrowing that would be necessary if inflation ended would consistently sustain indexing against opposition; not least, whether the apparent benefits of inflation have become so widespread and its dangers so obscured that it is unlikely to be mastered by voluntary decision and can be ended only by methods repugnant to a free society, of which incomes policies were a forerunner that failed because they were not enforced by increasingly authoritarian controls and sanctions.

There is much in the debate for students and teachers of economics, for people who make policy and who try to influence it in the press and broadcasting, and, not least, for the man in the street, whose happiness, fortune and perhaps liberty will be determined by its outcome. For all of them, this *Paper* may be an historic contribution to a debate that could decide whether the free society can master inflation or inflation will destroy the free society.

The Institute has to thank Professor Friedman for his prompt production of the manuscript, Mr Griffiths for writing his historical note at short notice, and the Editor of *Fortune* for material from his July 1974 number.

June 1974   EDITOR

[6]

The Author

MILTON FRIEDMAN was born in 1912 in New York City and graduated from Rutgers before taking MA at Chicago and PhD at Columbia. From 1935-37 he worked for the US National Resources Committee, from 1937-40 for the National Bureau of Economic Research, and from 1941-43 for the US Treasury. From 1946 to 1977 he taught at the University of Chicago, where in 1962 he became the Paul Snowden Russell Distinguished Service Professor of Economics.

Milton Friedman is now a Senior Research Fellow at the Hoover Institution of Stanford University. He has taught at universities throughout the world, from Cambridge to Tokyo. Since 1946 he has also been on the research staff of the National Bureau of Economic Research.

He is known to a wider audience as an advocate of a volunteer army (in place of the US draft), reverse income tax (in place of partial or universalist poverty programmes), monetary policy and floating exchange rates. He is the acknowledged head of the 'Chicago School' which specialises in the empirical testing of policy propositions derived from market analysis. Professor Friedman was awarded the 1976 Nobel Prize in Economic Sciences.

Among his best known books are *Essays in Positive Economics* (Chicago 1953), *Studies in the Quantity Theory of Money* (edited by Friedman, Chicago, 1956), *A Theory of the Consumption Function* (Princeton, 1957), *Capitalism and Freedom* (Chicago, 1962), (with Anna J. Schwartz) *A Monetary History of the United States, 1867-1960* (Princeton, 1963), and *The Optimum Quantity of Money* (Aldine, Chicago, and Macmillan, London, 1969). The IEA has published his Wincott Memorial Lecture, *The Counter-Revolution in Monetary Theory* (Occasional Paper 33, 1970, 4th impression 1978), *Monetary Correction* (Occasional Paper 41, 3rd impression 1978), *Unemployment versus Inflation?: An Evaluation of the Phillips Curve* (Occasional Paper 44, 3rd impression 1977), *From Galbraith to Economic Freedom* (Occasional Paper 49, 2nd impression 1977), and *Inflation and Unemployment: The New Dimension of Politics* (The 1976 Alfred Nobel Memorial Lecture, Occasional Paper 51, 2nd impression 1978); and his contributions to *Inflation: Causes, Consequences, Cures* (IEA Readings No. 14, 1974, 3rd impression 1976).

Monetary Correction

MILTON FRIEDMAN

Synopsis

THERE IS no technical problem about how to end inflation (Section I). The real obstacles are political, not technical.

Ending inflation would deprive government of revenue it now obtains without legislation (Section II). Replacing this revenue will require government to reduce expenditures, raise explicit taxes, or borrow additional sums from the public—all politically unattractive. I do not know any way to avoid this obstacle.

Political obstacles to ending inflation

Ending inflation would also have the side-effect of producing a temporary, though perhaps fairly protracted, period of economic recession or slowdown and of relatively high unemployment. The political will is today lacking to accept that side-effect. Experience suggests that its occurrence would instead produce an over-reaction involving accelerated government spending and monetary growth that in its turn would produce the initial side-effect of an unsustainable boom followed by accelerated inflation. These side-effects of changes in the rate of inflation arise because of the time it takes for the community to adjust itself to changed rates of growth of spending. The time-delay distorts relative prices, the structure of production and the level of employment. In turn, it takes time to correct these distortions (Section III).

The side-effects of changes in the rate of inflation can be substantially reduced by encouraging the widespread use of price escalator clauses in private and governmental contracts. Such arrangements involve deliberately eschewing some of the advantages of the use of money and hence are not good in and of themselves. They are simply a lesser evil than a badly-managed money. The widespread use of escalator clauses would not by itself either increase or decrease the rate of inflation. But it would reduce the revenue that government acquires from inflation—which also means that government would have less incentive to inflate. More important, it would reduce the

[9]

initial adverse side-effects on output and employment of effective measures to end inflation (Section IV).

Legal enforcement

The use of escalator clauses in government contracts—taxation, borrowing, hiring, purchasing—should be required by law. Their use in private contracts should be permitted and enforceable at law but should be voluntary. The two are related because government adoption of escalator clauses, particularly in taxes, would remove serious impediments to their private adoption (Section V).

Objections to widespread escalation mostly reflect misconceptions about its effects. These misconceptions reflect the same confusion between relative prices and absolute prices that is responsible for many of the adverse effects of accelerated inflation or deflation and for misconceptions about the cause and cure of inflation (Section VI).

I

THE TECHNICAL CAUSE AND CURE OF INFLATION

SHORT-RUN CHANGES in both particular prices and in the general level of prices may have many sources. But long-continued inflation is always and everywhere a monetary phenomenon that arises from a more rapid expansion in the quantity of money than in total output[1] —though I hasten to add that the exact rate of inflation is not precisely or mechanically linked to the exact rate of monetary growth. (The accompanying Chart (p. 11) plots consumer prices in Britain and the ratio of the quantity of money to output over the last decade.)

This statement is only a first step towards an understanding of the causes of any particular inflation. It must be completed by an explanation of the reason for the rapid monetary growth. The rapid monetary growth that produced inflation in the USA from 1848 to 1860 reflected gold discoveries in California. The rapid monetary growth that produced world inflation from 1890 to 1914 reflected the perfection of the cyanide process for extracting gold from low-grade ore. The rapid monetary growth that has time and again produced wartime inflation has reflected the use of the printing press or its equivalent to finance wartime government spending.

---

[1] This is a bit of an over-simplification, because a fully defensible statement would have to allow for autonomous changes in velocity, i.e., in the demand for real balances, and would have to specify the precise definition of 'money'. But I know of no case in which these qualifications are of critical importance.

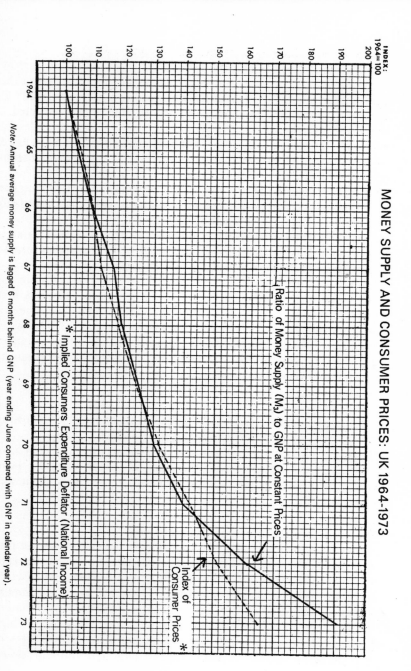

MONEY SUPPLY AND CONSUMER PRICES: UK 1964-1973

INDEX:
1964=100

Ratio of Money Supply (M₃) to GNP at Constant Prices

Index of Consumer Prices

* Implied Consumers' Expenditure Deflator (National Income)

Note: Annual average money supply is lagged 6 months behind GNP (year ending June compared with GNP in calendar year).

[11]

Causes of world-wide growth of money supply

Under modern conditions, the quantity of money is determined by governmental monetary authorities. The accelerated increase in the quantity of money throughout the world in the past decade, which is responsible for the recent acceleration of inflation, has reflected a number of causes:

(1) the attempt to maintain fixed exchange rates, which induced some countries, notably Germany and Japan, to 'import' inflation from the USA;

(2) the expansion in the role of government, and the reluctance to impose explicit taxes, which has induced many governments to use the implicit tax of inflation;

(3) the commitment of governments to a policy of full employment, which has led them to over-react to temporary recessions by measures leading to rapid monetary growth.

Long-continued inflation can be ended only by a reduction in the rate of monetary growth. But, again, this statement is only a first step. The measures that can be used to reduce the rate of monetary growth may vary widely depending on the sources of the excess growth and the institutions of the country in question. For example, if monetary growth has reflected the financing of government expenditures by the printing press, it can be ended by

(a) reducing government spending;

(b) raising taxes;

(c) financing the deficit in the government budget by borrowing from the public rather than by creating money.

But method (c) may not be available for a country that does not have well-developed security markets. And all hyper-inflations have reflected governments so impotent and disorganised as to be unable to employ (b).

Importance—and limitations—of fiscal policy

As these comments imply, fiscal policy may play an important role in producing and curing inflation. Its influence is primarily through its effect on the quantity of money. But its influence can be offset by other forces affecting the quantity of money. Large government surpluses in the USA in 1919 and 1920 did not prevent rapid inflation because they were accompanied by rapid monetary growth which financed private spending. Large government deficits in the USA in 1931 to 1933 did not produce rapid inflation or prevent severe deflation because they were accompanied by a sharp decline in the quantity of money which sharply reduced private spending.

What matters for inflation is not simply the rate of monetary growth but the rate of growth relative to the rate of growth of output, and, in a more sophisticated presentation, relative to the rate of growth in the demand for real money balances at a constant level (or rate of change) of prices. This relationship has led many commentators to emphasise the role of 'productivity', arguing that inflation reflects a decline in productivity (or its rate of growth) and that a cure requires an increase in productivity (or its rate of growth). Though the role of output growth is, in principle, strictly symmetrical to the role of monetary growth, the quantitative orders of magnitude are wholly different. For any given country, over any period longer than a few years, the rate of output growth is unlikely to vary by more than a few percentage points—it would take a major structural change, for example, to raise the rate of growth of output in the USA by two percentage points, from, say, 3–4 per cent per year to 5–6 per cent.[1] On the other hand, the rate of monetary growth can and does vary over a much wider range—it can easily go from 3 or 4 per cent per year to 20 per cent per year. As a matter of experience, therefore, long-continued inflation is dominated by monetary changes rather than by changes in output.

The importance of the simple proposition in this section is that no measures are likely to produce long-continued inflation or to cure long-continued inflation unless they affect the long-term rate of monetary growth.

II
GOVERNMENT REVENUE FROM INFLATION

SINCE TIME immemorial, the major source of inflation has been the sovereign's attempt to acquire resources to wage war, to construct monuments, or for other purposes. Inflation has been irresistibly attractive to sovereigns because it is a hidden tax that at first appears painless or even pleasant, and, above all, because it is a tax that can be imposed without specific legislation. It is truly taxation without representation.

---

[1] [In the UK the 1970–74 Conservative Government hoped to raise the annual rate of growth from 2.5–3 per cent in the late 1960s to 5 per cent. For a short period in 1972–73 it rose to 6¼ per cent (if the official measurements are reliable), but then fell to 4 per cent in 1973.—Ed.]

Three ways government gains from inflation

The revenue yield from inflation takes three major forms:

1. Additional government-created fiat money. Since ancient times, sovereigns have debased coinage by replacing silver or gold with base metals.[1] Later, paper currency supplemented token coins. More recently still, book entries at Central Banks (misleadingly called deposits) have been added. Governments use the fiat money that they issue to finance expenditures or repay debt. In addition, the fiat money serves as a base on which the banking system creates additional money in the form of bank deposits.

In the calendar year 1973 the US government realised $8,000 million (£3,300 million) from this source—$6,000 million (£2,500 million) additional currency and coin in circulation on 31 December, 1973 than on 31 December, 1972, and more than $2,000 million (£830 million) in additional deposits at Federal Reserve Banks.[2]

2. Inflation increases the yield of the personal and corporate income tax by pushing individuals and corporations into higher income groups, generating artificial (paper) capital gains on which taxes must be paid, and rendering permitted depreciation allowances inadequate to replace capital, so taxing a return *of* capital to shareholders as if it were a return *on* capital. For the corporation tax alone, the US government realised in 1973 nearly $13,000 million (£5,420 million) from this source.[3]

3. The reduction in the real amount of outstanding National Debt. Much of this debt was issued at yields that did not allow for current rates of inflation. On a conservative estimate, the US govern-

---

[1] One historian of money describes the debasement of the Roman *denarius* from an initially full-bodied silver coin until, by the time of Emperor Diocletian (300 AD), it had become 'practically a copper coin being only slightly washed with silver'. (Rupert J. Ederer, *The Evolution of Money*, Public Affairs Press, Washington, DC, 1964, p. 88.) We have gone further than Diocletian. We wash our copper coins now with nickel, so that not even a trace of silver remains.

[2] Excluding Treasury deposits. Nominally, the Federal Reserve Banks are owned by their member banks. This is a pure formality. In practice the Federal Reserve System is part of the government. It earns 'income' in the form of 'interest' paid to it by the US Treasury on government securities; it returns the excess of such 'interest' over operating expenses to the Treasury. Economic understanding is promoted and confusion avoided by consolidating the accounts of the Federal Reserve System with those of the Treasury.

[3] Inflation produced an over-statement of 1973 corporate profits by more than $26,000 million (£10,800 million) through spurious profits on stocks and under-depreciation, according to Department of Commerce estimates summarised by George Terborgh, *Inflation and Profits*, Machinery and Allied Products Institute (revised, 2 April, 1974). At a 48 per cent corporate tax rate, the additional tax paid was about $12,800 million (£5,300 million). In addition, corporate capital gains were undoubtedly over-stated.

ment realised in 1973 something like $5,000 million (£2,000 million) from this source.[1]

All told, the US government's revenue from inflation totalled more than $25,000 million (£10,000 million) in 1973. Ending inflation would end this source of revenue. Government would have to reduce expenditures, increase explicit taxes, or borrow additional funds from the public at whatever interest rate would clear the market. None of these courses is politically attractive.

III

SIDE-EFFECTS ON OUTPUT AND EMPLOYMENT

ACUTE APPENDICITIS is accompanied by a high fever; the removal of the appendix will require that the patient stay in bed for some days. But the fever is not the cause of the appendicitis and bed-rest is not the cure. Both are side-effects.

The analogy with inflation is striking. The boom that typically accompanies the onset of accelerated inflation is not the cause of the inflation but a side-effect; the recession and unemployment that typically accompany the reduction of inflation are not the cure but a side-effect. There are many ways to increase unemployment that would exacerbate inflation rather than cure it.

Time-lags lead to side-effects

Higher inflation reflects an acceleration in the growth rate of total money spending. Ending inflation requires a deceleration in the growth rate of total spending. The reason for the side-effects from such changes in total spending—both the boom which is generally regarded as a desirable side-effect and the recession which is uniformly regarded as an undesirable side-effect—is the time-delay between an increased or decreased rate of growth of total money spending and the full adjustment of output and prices to that changed rate of growth of total spending.

Essentially the same side-effects will arise whatever may be the cause of the changed growth rate in total spending—just as a high

---

[1] Total interest paid on the roughly $260,000 million (£108,000 million) of Federal debt held by the public was at an average rate of about 5.7 per cent. A 1973 market rate would have been about two percentage points higher, which means that the revenue to the government on this basis was about $5,000 million (£2,000 million). However, in retrospect, it seems clear that 1973 market rates did not adequately allow for inflation.

fever accompanies many different diseases and bed-rest many different cures. When non-monetary forces produce brief fluctuations in the rate of growth of total spending, the same side-effects occur. Also, if there is some cause other than unduly rapid monetary growth for long-continued inflation, or some cure other than reduced monetary growth, that cause and that cure will operate largely by affecting the growth rate in total money spending, and hence will produce much the same side-effects. Similarly, the measures proposed later to reduce the adverse side-effects of ending inflation will be effective whatever the cause and whatever the cure.

Hence the rest of this essay is relevant even if you do not accept my monetarist view as expressed in Section I.

Expectations slow to change

When total spending slows down, each producer separately tends to regard the reduction in the demand for his product as special to him, and to hope that it is temporary. He is inclined to meet it primarily by reducing output or accumulating stock, not by shading prices. Only after a time-lag will he start to shade prices. Similarly, any of his workers who are laid off are likely to react by waiting to be re-called or by seeking jobs elsewhere, not by moderating wage demands or expectations. A slowdown in total spending will therefore tend to be reflected initially in a widespread slowdown in output and employment and an increase in stocks. It will take some time before these responses lead in turn to widespread reductions in the rate of inflation and the rate of increase in wages. It will take still more time before *expectations* about inflation are revised and the revised expectations encourage a resumption of employment and output.

This is a highly simplified picture. Different activities have different time-speeds of adjustment. Some prices, wages and production schedules are fixed a long time in advance; others can be adjusted promptly. As a result, a slowdown of total spending produces substantial shifts in *relative* prices, which will sooner or later have to be corrected; the correction in turn will cause economic disturbances.

For the USA, study of monetary history[1] indicates that the time-delay between a change in the rate of monetary growth and a

[1] Milton Friedman, *The Optimum Quantity of Money*, Macmillan, London, 1969, Chapters 10, 11 and 12, and 'Letter on Monetary Policy', *Review*, Federal Reserve Bank of Saint Louis, March 1974. Also, A. James Meigs, *Money Matters*, Harper and Row, New York, 1972, Chapter 6.

corresponding change in the rate of growth of total spending and total output has averaged six to nine months; between the change in the rate of growth of spending and of prices, 12 to 18 months. Accordingly, the total delay between a change in monetary growth and in the rate of inflation has been about two years.[1] For the UK, the available evidence indicates that the time-delay is roughly the same as for the USA.

Serious effects on lending

The time-delay and resultant distortion are particularly clear for loans, where the distinction between *nominal* and *real* is especially important. Suppose you lend someone £100 in return for a promise to pay you £110 a year later. Neglect any possibility of default. What interest rate have you received? In pounds, 10 per cent. But if prices have risen by 10 per cent during the year, the £110 will buy only as much as the £100 would have done a year earlier. Your *real* return is nil. Indeed, if, as is true today, the £10 nominal return is subject to income tax, your *real* return is negative. You end up with *less* than you started with.

If you entered into a mortgage some years back, you may have paid 5 or 6 per cent. Given the inflation of the past few years, your effective *real* rate may have been nil. The rising price level probably raised the value of your property by as much as, or more than, the interest you paid. The lender in turn received a *real* return of nil—or a negative return if he was liable to tax. Similarly, consider someone who today takes out a mortgage at 11 per cent or more. Suppose economic policy were successful in bringing inflation down to nil. He would be in severe difficulties (unless of course the rate were reduced), and the lender would have received a wholly unexpected gain.

Failure of political will

Such side-effects constitute, I believe, the most important political obstacle to ending inflation, given, first, the commitment on the part of the US, UK and most other governments to 'full employment', secondly, the failure of the public at large to recognise the inevitable if temporary side-effects of ending inflation, and thirdly, the un-

[1] This is precisely what W. Stanley Jevons estimated it to be: 'An expansion of the currency occurs one or two years prior to a rise of prices.' (*Investigations into Currency and Finance*, Macmillan, 1884, p. 107.)

willingness or inability of political leaders to persuade the public to accept these side-effects.

Some years ago, when inflation was much lower than now, I believed that the re-adjustment required was sufficiently mild and brief to be politically feasible. But unfortunately in the USA the opportunity was cast aside on 15 August, 1971, when President Nixon reversed economic policy by imposing a price and wage freeze and encouraging expansive monetary and fiscal policy. At the time, we were well on the way to ending inflation without severe side-effects. At the cost of the mild 1970 recession, the annual rate of inflation had been reduced from over 6 per cent to 4.5 per cent and was still declining. The economy was slowly recovering from that recession. Had the nation had the will—for President Nixon was reflecting a widespread national consensus when he reversed policy—another year of continued monetary restraint and of slow expansion would probably have turned the trick. As it was, the 1970 recession was a masochistic exercise rather than a side-effect of a successful cure.

Inflation in the USA is currently (mid-1974) far worse than in August 1971. The 14 per cent rate in the first quarter of 1974 was doubtless a temporary bubble, but, even on the most optimistic view, inflation is not likely to fall below 6 per cent during the coming year. Starting from that level, and with inflationary expectations even more deeply entrenched, an effective policy to end inflation would entail as a side-effect a considerably more severe and protracted recession than we experienced in 1970. The political will to accept such a recession, without reversing policy and re-stimulating inflation, is simply not present.

What then? If we—and probably Britain and other countries similarly placed—do nothing, we shall suffer even higher rates of inflation—not continuously, but in spurts as we over-react to temporary recessions. Sooner or later, the public will get fed up, will demand effective action, and we shall then have a really severe recession.

IV

EASING THE SIDE-EFFECTS

How CAN we make it politically feasible to end inflation much sooner? As I see it, inflation can be ended sooner only by adopting measures that will reduce the side-effects from ending it. These side-effects fundamentally reflect distortions introduced into *relative* prices by *unanticipated* inflation or deflation, distortions that arise because contracts are entered into in terms of *nominal* prices under mistaken perceptions about the likely course of inflation.

Escalator clauses: an illustration
The way to reduce these side-effects is to make contracts in *real*, not nominal, terms. This can be done by the widespread use of escalator clauses.

Let me illustrate. In 1967 General Motors and the United Automobile Workers Union reached a wage agreement for a three-year period. At the time, prices had been relatively stable, consumer prices having risen at the average rate of 2.5 per cent in the preceding three years. The wage agreement was presumably based on an expectation by both General Motors and the union that prices would continue to rise at 2.5 per cent or less. That expectation was not realised. From 1967 to 1970, prices rose at an average annual rate of 5.2 per cent. The result was that General Motors paid *real* wages that were increasingly lower than the levels both parties had expected. The unexpected fall in real wages was a stimulus to General Motors, and no doubt led it to produce at a higher rate than otherwise. Initially, the unexpected fall in real wages was no deterrent to workers, since it took some time before they recognised that the accelerated rise in consumer prices was more than a transitory phenomenon. But by 1970 they were certainly aware that their real wages were less than they had bargained for.

The result was a strike in late 1970, settled by a wage agreement that provided (1) a very large increase in the initial year; (2) much smaller increases for the next two years; and (3) a cost-of-living escalator clause.

The contract was widely characterised as 'inflationary'. It was no such thing. The large initial year increase simply made up for the effect of the past unanticipated inflation. It restored *real wages* to the levels at which both parties had expected them to be. The escalator clause was designed to prevent a future similar distortion, and it has done so.

This General Motors example illustrates a side-effect of unanticipated inflation. Suppose the same contract had been reached in 1967 but that the rate of inflation, instead of accelerating, had declined from 2.5 per cent to nil. Real wages would then have risen above the level both parties had anticipated; General Motors would have been driven to reduce output and employment; the workers would have welcomed the unexpectedly high real wage-rate but would have deplored the lower employment; when contract renewal was due, the union, not General Motors, would have been in a weak bargaining position.

An escalator clause which works both up and down would have prevented both the actual side-effects from unanticipated inflation and the hypothetical side-effects from unanticipated deflation. It would have enabled employers and employees to bargain in terms of the conditions of their own industry without having also to guess what was going to happen to prices in general, because both General Motors and the union would have been protected against either more rapid inflation or less rapid inflation.

Useful though they are, widespread escalator clauses are not a panacea. It is impossible to escalate *all* contracts (consider, for example, paper currency), and costly to escalate many. A powerful advantage of using money is precisely the ability to carry on transactions cheaply and efficiently, and universal escalator clauses reduce this advantage. Far better to have no inflation and no escalator clauses. But that alternative is not currently available.

Origins of the escalator: the 'tabular standard'

Let me note also that the widespread use of escalator clauses is not a new or untried idea. It dates back to at least 1707, when a Cambridge don, William Fleetwood, estimated the change in prices over a 600-year period in order to calculate comparable limits on outside income that college Fellows were permitted to receive. It was suggested explicitly in 1807 by an English writer on money, John Wheatley. It was spelled out in considerable detail and recommended enthusiastically in 1886 by the great English economist, Alfred Marshall.[1] The great American economist Irving Fisher not only favoured the 'tabular standard'—as the proposal for widespread indexation was labelled nearly two centuries ago—but also persuaded a manufacturing company that he helped to found to issue a purchasing-power security as long ago as 1925. Interest in the 'tabular standard' was the major factor accounting for the development of

---

[1] His discussion is reproduced in a Note to this *Paper*, below, p. 33

index numbers of prices. In recent years, the 'tabular standard' has been adopted by Brazil on a wider scale than I would recommend for the USA. It has been adopted on a smaller scale by Canada, Israel, and many other countries.[1]

<h2 style="text-align:center">V</h2>

<h3 style="text-align:center">THE SPECIFIC PROPOSAL</h3>

FOR THE USA, my specific proposal has two parts, one for the Federal government, one for the rest of the economy. For the Federal government, I propose that escalator clauses be legislated; for the rest of the economy, that they be voluntary but that any legal obstacles be removed. The question of which index number to use in such escalator clauses is important but not critical. As Alfred Marshall said in 1886, 'A perfectly exact measure of purchasing power is not only unattainable, but even unthinkable'. For the USA, as a matter of convenience, I would use the cost-of-living index number calculated by the Bureau of Labour Statistics.

(a) *The Government*[2]
The US government has already adopted escalation for social security payments, retirement benefits to Federal employees, wages of many government employees, and perhaps some other items. Taxes which are expressed as fixed percentages of price or other value base are escalated automatically. The key additional requirement is for escalator clauses in the personal and corporate income tax and in government securities.

The personal tax. Minor details aside, four revisions are called for:
(i) The personal exemption, the standard deduction, and the low income allowance should be expressed not as a given number of dollars, but as a given number of dollars multiplied by the ratio of a price index for the year in question to the index for the base year in which 'indexation' starts. For example, if in the first

---

[1] A useful survey is in Robert P. Collier, *Purchasing Power Bonds and Other Escalated Contracts*, Buffalo Book Co., Taipei, Taiwan, 1969 (distributed in the USA by the Utah State University Press, Logan, Utah).
    [The British Government began to review pensions and other social benefits annually in the light of rising prices in 1973 and the Conservative Party promised revision twice a year in its 1974 election manifesto.—Ed.]
[2] [In principle, with change of detail, these observations apply, or could apply, to Britain. Cf. the note on 'Fiscal Drag and Inflation', below, p. 49.—Ed.]

year prices rise by 10 per cent, then the present amounts should be multiplied by 110/100 or 1.10.

(ii) The brackets in the tax tables should be adjusted similarly, so that, in the examples given, 0–$500 would become 0–$550, and so on.

(These two measures have been adopted by Canada.)

(iii) The base for calculating capital gains should be multiplied by the ratio of the price index in the year of sale to the price index in the year of purchase. This would prevent the taxing of non-existent, purely paper capital gains.

(iv) The base for calculating depreciation on fixed capital assets should be adjusted in the same way as the base for calculating capital gains.

The corporate tax.[1]

(i) The present $25,000 (£10,400) dividing line between normal tax and surtax should be replaced by that sum multiplied by a price index number.

(ii) The cost of stocks used in sales should be adjusted to eliminate book profits (or losses) resulting from changes in prices between initial purchase and final sale.

The base for calculating (iii) capital gains, and (iv) depreciation of fixed capital assets should be adjusted as for the personal tax.

Government securities.[1] Except for short-term bills and notes, all government securities should be issued in purchasing-power form. (For example, Series E bonds should promise a redemption value equal to the product of the face value calculated at, say, 3 per cent per year and the ratio of the price index in the year of redemption to the price index in the year of purchase.) Coupon securities should carry coupons redeemable for the face amount multiplied by the relevant price ratio, and bear a maturity value equal to the face amount similarly multiplied by the relevant price ratio.

These changes in taxes and in borrowing would reduce both the incentive for government to resort to inflation and the side-effects of changes in the rate of inflation on the private economy. But they are called for also by elementary principles of ethics, justice, and representative government, which is why I propose making them permanent.

---

[1] These tax and borrowing measures are all contained in a Bill introduced by Senator James Buckley in April 1974.

Taxation inflated to record levels

As a result largely of inflation produced by government in the USA, the UK and elsewhere, personal income taxes are today heavier than during the peak of Second World War financing, despite several 'reductions' in tax rates. Personal exemptions in real terms are at a record low level. The taxes levied on persons in different economic circumstances deviate widely from the taxes explicitly intended to apply to them. Government has been in the enviable position of imposing higher taxes while appearing to reduce taxes. The less enviable result has been a wholly arbitrary distribution of the higher taxes.

As for government borrowing, the savings bond campaigns of the US and UK Treasuries have been the largest bucket-shop operations ever engaged in.[1] This is not a recent development. In responding to a questionnaire of the Joint Economic Committee of Congress, I wrote as early as 1951:

> 'I strongly favour the issuance of a purchasing-power bond on two grounds: (a) It would provide a means for lower- and middle-income groups to protect their capital against the ravages of inflation. This group has almost no effective means of doing so now. It seems to me equitable and socially desirable that they should. (b) It would permit the Treasury to sell bonds without engaging in advertising and promotion that at best is highly misleading, at worst, close to being downright immoral. The Treasury urges people to buy bonds as a means of securing their future. Is the implicit promise one that it can make in good faith, in light of past experience of purchasers of such bonds who have seen their purchasing power eaten away by price rises? If it can be, there is no cost involved in making the promise explicit by adding a purchasing-power guarantee. If it cannot be, it seems to me intolerable that an agency of the public deliberately mislead the public.'

Surely the experience of the nearly quarter-century since these

---

[1] [In the UK the *Report* of the Committee to Review National Savings (the Page Committee: Cmnd. 5273, HMSO, June 1973) found that 'the £9,546 million of National Savings invested at the end of March 1972 was worth only £4,269 million if expressed in the purchasing power of money in March 1951. Since the total value of National Savings at end March 1951 was £6,130 million, in real terms National Savings are contracting' (para. 568). It therefore examined the arguments for and against index-linking for government securities and concluded that 'an experiment should be undertaken of issuing a modest index-linked bond for the small saver on the grounds that he is least able to protect his capital against inflation' (para. 583).—Ed.]

words were written reinforces their pertinence. Essentially every purchaser of savings bonds or, indeed, almost any other long-term Treasury security during that period, has paid for the privilege of lending to the government: the supposed 'interest' he has received has not compensated for the decline in the purchasing power of the principal, and, to add insult to injury, he has had to pay tax on the paper interest. And the inflation which has sheared the innocent lambs has been produced by the government which benefits from the shearing.

It is a mystery to me—and a depressing commentary on either the understanding or the sense of social responsibility of businessmen (I say business *men*, not business)—that year after year eminent and honourable business leaders have been willing to aid and abet this bucket-shop operation by joining committees to promote the sale of US saving bonds or by providing facilities for payroll deductions for their employees who buy them.

(b) *The Private Economy*

Private use of escalator clauses is an expedient that has no permanent role, if government manages money responsibly. Hence I favour keeping private use voluntary in order to promote its self-destruction if that happy event arrives.

No legislation is required for the private adoption of escalator clauses, which are now widespread. Something over 5 million US workers[1] are covered by union contracts with automatic escalator clauses, and there must be many non-union workers who have similar implicit or explicit agreements with their employers. Many contracts for future delivery of products contain provisions for adjustment of the final selling price either for specific changes in costs or for general price changes. Many rental contracts for business premises are expressed as a percentage of gross or net receipts, which means that they have an implicit escalator clause. This is equally true for percentage royalty payments and for automobile insurance policies that pay the cost of repairing damage. Some insurance companies issue fire insurance policies the face value of which is automatically adjusted for inflation. No doubt there are many more examples of which I am ignorant.

[1] [Eight to nine million in the UK where threshold agreements have been widely adopted since they received the Conservative Government's sanction in its counter-inflation policy: *The price and pay code for Stage 3. A consultative document*, Cmnd. 5444, HMSO, Autumn 1973.—Ed.]

It is highly desirable that escalator clauses should be incorporated in a far wider range of wage agreements, contracts for future delivery of products, and financial transactions involving borrowing and lending. The first two are entirely straightforward extensions of existing practices. The third is more novel.

'Indexation' for corporate loans

The arrangements suggested for government borrowing would apply equally to long-term borrowing by private enterprises. Instead of issuing a security promising to pay, say, interest of 9 per cent per year and to repay £1,000 at the end of five years, the XYZ company could promise to pay 3 per cent plus the rate of inflation each year and to repay £1,000 at the end of five years. Alternatively, it could promise to pay each year 3 per cent times the ratio of the price index in that year to the price index in the year the security was issued and to repay at the end of five years £1,000 times the corresponding price ratio for the fifth year. (The alternative methods are illustrated in Table I.) If there is inflation, the first method implicitly involves amortising part of the real value of the bond over the five-year period; the second involves currently paying interest only, at a constant real rate, and repaying the whole principal in *real* value at the end of the five years.

TABLE I
Hypothetical Indexed Bond
£1,000 five-year bond issued in 1968 at a real rate of 3 per cent

Year	UK Consumer Index (1968 = 100)	Price Level Percentage change	Payments each year Method 1	Method 2
			Interest	
			£	£
1968	100			
1969	105.2	5.2	82	31.56
1970	112.0	6.5	95	33.60
1971	122.6	9.5	125	36.78
1972	131.0	6.8	98	39.60
1973	142.0	8.4	114	42.60
			Principal	
			£1,000	£1,420

So far, there has been little incentive for private borrowers to issue such securities. The delay in adjusting anticipations about

[25]

inflation to the actual acceleration of inflation has meant that interest rates on long-term bonds have been extremely low in real terms. Almost all enterprises that have issued bonds in the past decade have done extremely well—the rate of inflation has often exceeded the interest rate they had to pay, making the real cost negative.

Lenders' changing expectations

Three factors could change this situation.

(1) As lenders, who have been the losers so far, come to have more accurate expectations of inflation, borrowers will have to pay rates high enough to compensate for the actual inflation.

(2) Government purchasing-power securities might prove so attractive that competition would force private enterprises to do the same.

(3) Related to (2), if it became clear that there was a real possibility that government would follow effective policies to stem inflation, borrowing would no longer be a one-way street. Enterprises would become concerned that they might become locked into high-interest rate loans. They might then have more interest in protecting themselves against inflation.

Businessmen's fears unwarranted

One question has invariably been raised when I have discussed this possibility with corporate executives: 'Is it not too risky for us to undertake an open-ended commitment? At least with fixed nominal rates we know what our obligations are'. This is a natural query from business men reared in an environment in which a roughly stable price level was taken for granted. But in a world of *varying* rates of inflation, the *fixed*-rate agreement is the more risky agreement. To quote Alfred Marshall again,

'Once it [the tabular standard] has become familiar none but gamblers would lend or borrow on any other terms, at all events for long periods.'

The money receipts of most businesses vary with inflation. If inflation is high, their receipts in money terms are high and they can pay the escalated rate of interest; if inflation is low, their receipts are low and they will find it easier to pay the low rate with the adjustment

[26]

for inflation than a fixed but high rate; and similarly at the time of redemption.

The crucial point is the relation between assets and liabilities. Currently, for many enterprises, their assets, including goodwill, are real in the sense that their money value will rise or fall with the general price level; but their liabilities tend to be nominal, i.e. fixed in money terms. Accordingly, these enterprises benefit from inflation at a higher rate than was anticipated when the nominal liabilities were acquired and are harmed by inflation at a lower rate than was anticipated. If assets and liabilities were to match, such enterprises would be protected against either event.

Home mortgages—threat of 'major crisis'

A related yet somewhat different case is provided by financial intermediaries. Consider savings and loan associations and mutual savings banks. Both their assets (primarily home mortgages) and their liabilities (due to shareholders or depositors) are expressed in money terms. But they differ in time duration. The liabilities are in practice due on demand;[1] the assets are long-term. The current mortgages were mostly issued when inflation, and therefore interest rates, were much lower than they are now. If the mortgages were re-valued at current yields, i.e. at the market prices for which they could be sold in a free secondary market, every US savings and loan association would be technically insolvent.

So long as the thrift institutions can maintain their level of deposits, no problem arises because they do not have to liquidate their assets. But if inflation speeds up, interest rates on market instruments will rise further. Unless the thrift institutions offer competitive interest rates, their shareholders or depositors will withdraw funds to get a better yield (the process inelegantly termed 'disintermediation'). But with their income fixed, the thrift institutions will find it difficult or impossible to pay competitive rates. This situation is concealed but not altered by the legal limits on the rates they are permitted to pay.

Further acceleration of inflation threatens a major crisis for this group of financial institutions. And the crisis is no minor matter. Total assets of these US institutions approach $400,000 million (£167,000 million).[2] As it happens, they would be greatly helped by a

---

[1] [Or, in Britain, at short notice.—Ed.]
[2] [British building society assets exceed £17,500 million.—Ed.]

[27]

deceleration of inflation, but some of their recent borrowers who are locked into high rates on mortgages would be seriously hurt.[1]

Benefits of inflation-proofed loans

Consider how different the situation of the thrift institutions would be with widespread escalator clauses: the mortgages on their books would be yielding, say, 5 per cent plus the rate of inflation; they could afford to pay to their shareholders or depositors, say, 3 or 4 per cent plus the rate of inflation. They, their borrowers, and their shareholders or depositors would be fully protected against changes in the rate of inflation. They would be assuming risks only with respect to the much smaller possible changes in the *real* rate of interest rather than in the money rate.

Similarly an insurance company could afford to offer an inflation-protected policy if its assets were in inflation-protected loans to business or in mortgages or government securities. A pension fund could offer inflation-protected pensions if it held inflation-protected assets. In Brazil, where this practice has, to my knowledge, been carried furthest, banks are required to credit a 'monetary correction' equal to the rate of inflation on all time deposits and to charge a 'monetary correction' on all loans extending beyond some minimum period.

To repeat, none of these arrangements is without cost. It would be far better if stable prices made them unnecessary. But they seem to me far less costly than continuing on the road to periodic acceleration of inflation, ending in a real bust.

The suggested governmental arrangements would stimulate the private arrangements. Today, one deterrent to issuing private purchasing-power securities is that the inflation adjustment would be taxable to the recipient along with the real interest paid. The proposed tax changes would in effect exempt such adjustments from taxation, and so make purchasing-power securities more attractive to lenders. In addition, government issues of purchasing-power securities would offer effective competition to private borrowers, inducing them to follow suit, and would provide assets that could be used as the counterpart of inflation-protected liabilities.

Prospects for private contract escalators

Would escalator clauses spread in private contracts? That depends

---

[1] [Unless interest rates are lowered, as they would be in Britain.—Ed.]

Monetary Correction: The British Context

To illustrate the relevance of Professor Friedman's analysis for the British economy we add Charts on the main indicators (and Tables on pp. 52–54).—Ed.

CHART 1

MONEY SUPPLY · UK

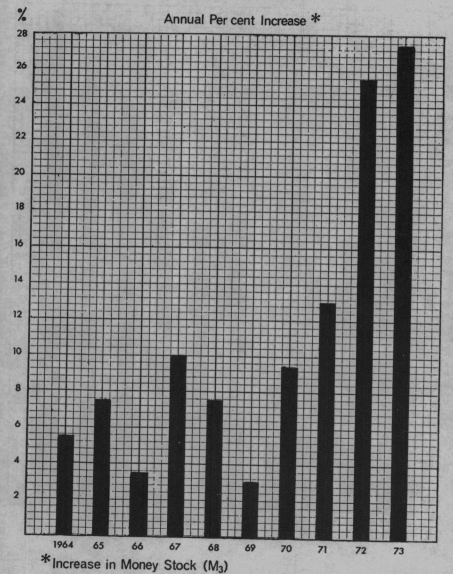

%

Annual Per cent Increase *

* Increase in Money Stock (M₃)

I

CHART 2

WEEKLY EARNINGS IN INDUSTRY: UK

Annual Per cent Increase

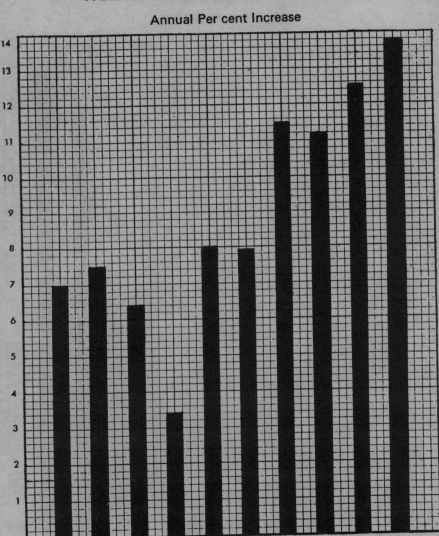

II

CHART 3

RETAIL PRICES: UK

Annual Per cent Increase 1964-1974

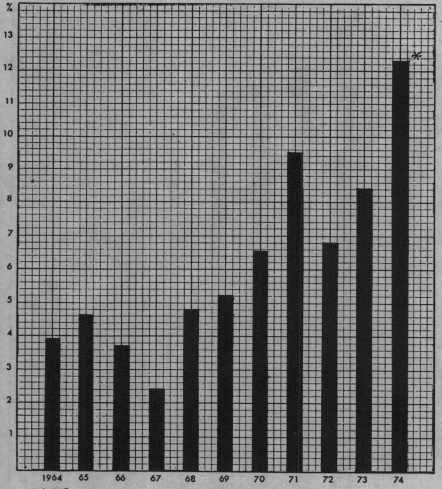

* 1st Quarter compared with 1st Quarter 1973

III

CHART 4

PRICE INCREASE IN UK AND OTHER COUNTRIE.

Per cent Increase in Consumer Prices 1970-1973

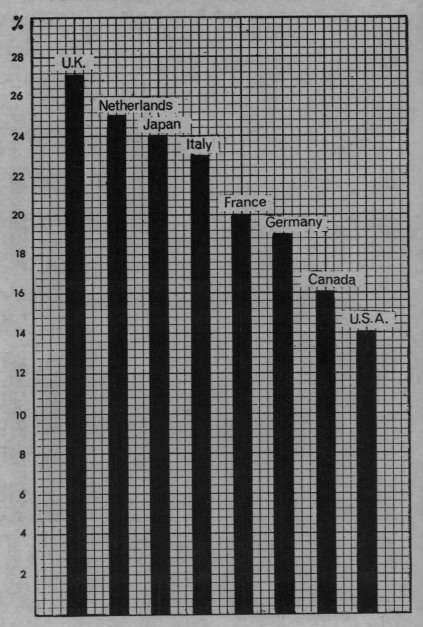

IV

on the course of inflation. If, by some miracle, inflation were to disappear in the near future, all talk of such arrangements would also disappear. The more likely development is that US inflation will taper off in late 1974, will settle at something like 6 or 7 per cent in 1975, and will then start to accelerate in 1976 in response to the delayed impact of over-reaction in 1974 to rising unemployment. During this period there will be a steady but unspectacular expansion of escalator clauses. If inflation accelerates to 10 per cent and beyond in 1977 or so, the steady expansion will turn into a bandwagon.

Needless to say, I hope this scenario is wrong. I hope that the Federal Reserve and the Administration will be willing and able to resist the pressure to over-react to the 1974 recession, that they will maintain fiscal and monetary restraint, and so avoid another acceleration of inflation. But neither past experience, nor the present political climate, makes that hope a reasonable expectation.

Making it easier to fight inflation
How would widespread adoption of the escalator principle affect economic policy? Some critics say indexation would condemn us to perpetual inflation. I believe that, on the contrary, indexation would enhance government's ability to act against inflation.

To begin with, indexation will temper some of the hardships and distortions that now follow from a drop in the rate of inflation. Employers will not be stuck with excessively high wage increases under existing union contracts, for wage increases will moderate as inflation recedes. Borrowers will not be stuck with excessively high interest costs, for the rates on outstanding loans will moderate as inflation recedes. Indexation will also partly counteract the tendency of businesses to defer capital investment once total spending begins to decline—there will be less reason to wait in expectation of lower prices and lower interest rates. Businesses will be able to borrow funds or enter into construction contracts knowing that interest rates and contract prices will be adjusted later in accord with indexes of prices.

Most important, indexation will shorten the time it takes for a reduction in the rate of growth of total spending to have its full effect in reducing the rate of inflation. As the deceleration of demand pinches at various points in the economy, any effects on prices will be transmitted promptly to wage contracts, contracts for future

[29]

delivery, and interest rates on outstanding long-term loans. Accordingly, producers' wage costs and other costs will go up less rapidly than they would without indexation. This tempering of costs, in turn, will encourage employers to keep more people on the payroll, and produce more goods, than they would without indexation. The encouragement of supply, in turn, will work against price increases, with additional moderating feedback on wages and other costs.

With widespread indexation, in sum, firm monetary restraint by the Federal Reserve System (the 'Fed') would be reflected in a much more even reduction in the pace of inflation and a much smaller transitory rise in unemployment. The success in slowing inflation would steel political will to suffer the smaller withdrawal pains and so might make it possible for the 'Fed' to persist in a firm policy. As it became credible that the 'Fed' would persist, private reactions could reinforce the effects of its policy. The economy would move to non-inflationary growth at high levels of employment much more rapidly than now seems possible.

VI

OBJECTIONS TO ESCALATOR CLAUSES

THE MAJOR objection to widespread escalation is the allegation that escalators have an inflationary impact on the economy.[1] In this simple-minded form, the statement is simply false—as I noted earlier in connection with the 1970 General Motors settlement. An escalator goes into effect only as the *result* of a *previous* price increase. Whence came that? An escalator can go down as well as up. If inflation slows, and hence so do wage increases, do escalators have a *deflationary* impact?

In the first instance, escalators have *no* direct effect on the rate of inflation. They simply assure that inflation affects different prices and wages alike and thus avoid the kind of distortions in relative prices and wages illustrated by the General Motors case. With widespread escalation, inflation would be *transmitted* more quickly and evenly, and hence the harm done by inflation would be less. But why should that raise or lower the *rate* of inflation?

[1] [A Treasury Minister in the 1970–74 Conservative Government has argued that those who advocate indexation are 'arguing that one ought to try to live with inflation rather than control it, which I regard as a dangerous point from which to start'. (Mr Terence Higgins, *Hansard*, 20 May, 1974, col. 83.)—Ed.]

Incentive to raise tax rates?

Two objections have been made on a more sophisticated level. First, widespread escalation would restrict the government revenue from inflation simply to the direct tax on cash balances produced by the issue of additional high-powered money (point (1), p. 14). It would thereby reduce the revenue from a given rate of inflation, which could induce government to raise the rate of tax.

'Living with inflation'

Second, the general public could interpret the adoption of escalator clauses as demonstrating that the government has given up the fight against inflation, and is seeking only to 'live with inflation'. This might lead the public to raise its own anticipations of future inflation, which, by reducing its willingness to hold cash balances, could cause a once-for-all rise in the price level and to that extent be a self-fulfilling prophecy.

Neither objection seems to me weighty. If the public does not wish to stop inflation but is content to allow government to use inflation as a regular source of revenue, the sooner we adapt our institutions to that situation the better. Similarly, the second objection has little relevance to the proposal for escalator clauses as a means for removing *political* obstacles to ending inflation.

On a still more sophisticated level, it can be argued that, by removing distortions in relative prices produced by inflation, widespread escalator clauses would make it easier for the public to recognise changes in the rate of inflation, would thereby reduce the time-lag in adapting to such changes, and thus make the nominal price level more sensitive and variable. This is certainly possible, though by no means demonstrated. But, if so, the *real variables* would be made *less* sensitive and *more* stable—a highly beneficial trade-off. Moreover, it is also possible that, by making accurate estimates of the rate of inflation less important, widespread escalator clauses would reduce the attention devoted to such estimates, and thereby provide more stability.

An objection of a very different kind is that inflation serves the critical social purpose of resolving incompatible demands by different groups. To put it crudely, the participants in the economy have 'non-negotiable demands' for more than the whole output. These demands are reconciled because inflation fools people into believing that their demands have been met when in fact they have not been, nominal returns being eroded by unanticipated inflation.

Escalator clauses, it is argued, bring the inconsistent demands into the open. Workers who would accept a lower real wage produced by unanticipated inflation will not be willing to accept the same real wage in explicit negotiations.[1] If this view is correct on a wide enough scale to be important, I see no ultimate outcome other than either runaway inflation or an authoritarian society ruled by force. Perhaps it is only wishful thinking that makes me reluctant to accept this vision of our fate.

VII

CONCLUSION

THE CONVENTIONAL political wisdom is that the citizenry may mutter about inflation but votes on the basis of the level of unemployment. Nobody, it is said, has ever lost an election because of inflation: Hoover in 1932 and Nixon in 1960 lost because of unemployment.

As we leave the depression decade farther and farther behind, and as we experience more and more inflation, this conventional wisdom becomes increasingly questionable. Inflation surely helped to make Mr Edward Heath Prime Minister in 1970 and, even more surely, ex-Prime Minister in 1974. The popularity of Japan's Prime Minister, Mr K. Tanaka, is at an all-time low because of inflation. President Allende of Chile lost his life at least partly because of inflation. Throughout the world, inflation is a major source of political unrest.

Perhaps widespread escalator clauses are not the best expedient in this time of trouble. But I know of no other that has been suggested that holds out as much promise of both reducing the harm done by inflation and facilitating the ending of inflation. If inflation continues to accelerate, the conventional political wisdom will be reversed. The insistence on ending inflation at whatever cost will lead to a severe depression. Now, before that has occurred, is the time to take measures that will make it politically feasible to end inflation before inflation ends not only the conventional wisdom but perhaps also the free society.

[1] [This is essentially the 'money illusion' behind Keynes's view that workers would not accept lower money wages but would accept lower real wages resulting from unchanged (or even rising) money wages reduced in real value by rising prices (inflation). —Ed.]

The British Background

1. A CLASSICAL FORERUNNER:

ALFRED MARSHALL ON THE 'TABULAR STANDARD'[1]

I AGREE with the general opinion that a steady upward tendency in general prices conduces a little more to the general well-being than does a tendency downwards, because it keeps industry somewhat better employed. But, on the other hand, people of all classes, and especially of the working classes, spend their incomes more wisely when prices and money-wages are falling, and they think themselves worse off than they are, than when a rise of prices and money-wages leads them to exaggerate their real incomes and to be careless about their expenditure. So that, on the whole, I think there is much less difference than is generally supposed between the net benefits of periods of rising and falling prices. It is doubtful whether the last ten years, which are regarded as years of depression, but in which there have been few violent movements of prices, have not, on the whole, conduced more to solid progress and true happiness than the alternations of feverish activity and painful retrogression which have characterised every preceding decade of this century. In fact, I regard violent fluctuations of prices as a much greater evil than a gradual fall of prices. I will venture to quote a passage from a paper on remedies for the discontinuity of industry, which I read last year at the 'Industrial Remuneration Conference':

'A great cause of the discontinuity of industry is the want of certain knowledge as to what a pound is going to be worth a short time hence. With every expansion and contraction of credit prices rise and fall. This change of prices presses heavily even on those who kept themselves as far as possible from the uncertainties of trade, and increases in many ways the intensity of commercial fluctuations. For just when private traders and public companies are most inclined to reckless ventures, the interest which they have to pay on borrowed capital represents an exceptionally small purchasing power, because prices are high. And in the opposite phase, when their resources are

[1] Extract from 'Reply to the Royal Commission on the Depression of Trade and Industry' (1886), reproduced in *Official Papers by Alfred Marshall*, Macmillan, London, 1926.

crippled by the stagnation of business the lowness of prices compels them to sacrifice a much greater amount of real wealth in order to pay their interest. When traders are rejoicing in high prices debenture and mortgage holders and other creditors are depressed; and when the pendulum swings the other way traders, already depressed, are kept under water by having to pay an exceptionally heavy toll to their creditors. This serious evil can be much diminished by a plan which economists have long advocated. In proposing this remedy I want Government to help business, though not to do business. It should publish tables showing as closely as may be the changes in the purchasing power of gold, and should facilitate contracts for payments to be made in terms of units of fixed purchasing power.

'Government already does work of the kind desired in regard to the tithe commutation tables. But instead of dealing with wheat, barley, and oats, it would deal with all important commodities. It would publish their prices once a month or once a year; it would reckon the importance of each commodity as proportioned to the total sum spent on it, and then by simple arithmetic deduce the change in the purchasing power of gold. Borrowings could then, at the option of the contracting parties, be reckoned in Government units. On this plan, if A lends B 1,000*l.* at 4½ per cent interest, and after some years the purchasing power of money had risen by an eighth, B would have to pay as interest, not 45*l.*, but a sum that had the same purchasing power as 45*l.* had at the time of borrowing, i.e. 40*l.*, and so on. The plan would have to win its way into general use, but when once it had become familiar none but gamblers would lend or borrow on any other terms, at all events for long periods. The scheme has no claims to theoretic perfection, but only to being a great improvement on our present methods, and obtained with little trouble. A perfectly exact measure of purchasing power is not only unattainable, but even unthinkable. The same change of prices affects the purchasing power of money to different persons in different ways. For to him who can seldom afford to have meat, a fall of one-fourth in the price of meat accompanied by a rise of one-fourth in that of bread means a fall in the purchasing power of money; his wages will not go so far as before. While to his richer neighbour, who spends twice as much on meat as on bread, the change acts the other way. The Government would, of course, take account only of the total consumption of the whole nation; but even so it would be troubled by constant changes in the way in which the

[34]

nation spent its income. The estimate of the importance of different commodities would have to be recast from time to time. The only room for differences of opinion would be as to what commodities should be taken account of. It would probably be best to follow the ordinary method of taking very little account of any but raw commodities. Manufactured commodities and personal services are always changing their character, and are not easily priced. Manufactured tend to fall in value relatively to raw commodities, and at present, at all events, personal services tend to rise, so that the errors made by omitting both probably nearly neutralise one another. Simplicity and definiteness are in this case far more important than theoretic accuracy. Those who make the returns should work in the open day, so that they could not, if they would, be subject to many influences. This plan, though strange at first sight, would really be much simpler than bimetallism, while its influence in steadying industry would be incomparably greater.'

The task of publishing from time to time the currency value of a unit of constant purchasing power cannot, I think, be performed properly except by a permanent Government department. So far as the exports and imports go, the materials for this have been provided by the Board of Trade. Their work is a perfect model of method, which cannot fail to be of use to us; but it is not directly applicable to our present purpose. In Mr Palgrave's memorandum a most interesting example is shown of the kind of index-number that is wanted. But Government alone can command the machinery requisite to secure properly tested figures for the purpose.

The unit of constant general purchasing power would be applicable, at the free choice of both parties concerned, for nearly all contracts for the payment of interest, and for the repayment of loans; and for many contracts for rent, and for wages and salaries. But as people became more familiar with the plan, certain modifications might gradually be made, again by the consent of those concerned, for special cases. For instance, there might be an agricultural unit, either suggested directly by the Government or adapted by private persons from the figures supplied by the Government. This unit would be got from the general unit by increasing the weight of the prices of agricultural produce. It might be agreed that while the total amounts spent on other things should be taken as they are, every 1,000,000*l.* spent on agricultural produce should be treated for this special purpose as though it were (say) 4,000,000*l.* This plan would,

I think, be fairer, and, when once thoroughly understood, more popular, than the plan which has been proposed of fixing agricultural rents at the price of a certain amount of farm produce. Again, by a similar modification, a mining unit might be got which would supersede the useful but not quite satisfactory sliding scales that are adopted at present; and so for other trades.

I wish to emphasise the fact that this proposal is independent of the form of our currency, and does not ask for any change in it. I admit that the plan would seldom be available for the purposes of international trade. But its importance as a steadying influence to our home trade would be so great, and its introduction would be so easy and so free from the evils which generally surround the interference of Government in business, that I venture to urge strongly its claims on your immediate attention. . . .

ALFRED MARSHALL ON

A STANDARD OF VALUE INDEPENDENT OF GOLD AND SILVER[1]

. . . LEAVING SOME difficulties of detail to be discussed at the end of the article, let us suppose that (as was suggested long ago by Joseph Lowe, Poulett Scrope and others)[2] a Government Department extends to all commodities the action taken by the Commissioners of Tithes with regard to wheat, barley and oats. As they, having ascertained the average prices of grain at any time, state how much money is required to purchase as much wheat, barley and oats as would have cost £100 at certain standard prices, so this Department, having ascertained the prices of all important commodities, would publish from time to time the amount of money required to give the same general purchasing power, as, say, £1 had at the beginning of 1887. The prices used by it would be the latest attainable; not, as in the case of tithes, the mean of the prices for the last seven years. This standard unit of purchasing power might be called for shortness simply THE UNIT.

From time to time, at the beginning of each year or oftener, the Department would declare how much of the currency had the same purchasing power as £1 had at the beginning of 1887. If, for instance,

---

[1] Extract from 'Remedies for Fluctuations of General Prices' (1887), *Memorials of Alfred Marshall*, ed. A. C. Pigou, Macmillan, 1925, pp. 197–199.
[2] Some account of their suggestions is given in the chapter on 'A Tabular Standard of Value' in Jevons's *Money*.

it declared in 1890 that 18s. had this purchasing power, then a contract to pay a unit in 1890 would be discharged by paying 18s. If it declared in 1892 that 23s. had only the same purchasing power as £1 had in 1887, or 18s. in 1890, then any contract to pay a unit in 1892 would require for its settlement the delivery of 23s.

When a loan was made, it could, at the option of those concerned, be made in terms of currency, or in terms of units. In the latter case the lender would know that whatever change there might be in the value of money, he would receive when the debt was repaid just the same amount of real wealth, just the same command over the necessaries, comforts and luxuries of life as he had lent away. If he bargained for 5 per cent interest, he would each year receive money equal in value to one-twentieth of the units which he had lent; and however prices might have changed, these would contribute a certain and definite amount to his real means of expenditure. The borrower would not be at one time impatient to start ill-considered enterprises in order to gain by the expected rise in general prices, and at another afraid of borrowing for legitimate business for fear of being caught by a general fall in prices.

Of course every trade would still have its own dangers due to causes peculiar to itself; but by the use of the unit it might avoid those heavy risks which are caused by a rise or fall in general prices. Salaries and wages, where not determined by special sliding scales, could be fixed in units, their real value would then no longer fluctuate constantly in the wrong direction, tending upwards just when, if it changed at all, it should fall, and tending downwards just when, if it changed at all, it should rise.[1]

Ground-rents also should be fixed in general units, though for agricultural rents it would be best to have a special unit based chiefly on the prices of farm produce. The reckoning of mortgages and marriage settlements in terms of units of purchasing power, instead of gold, would remove one great source of uncertainty from the affairs of private life, while a similar change as to debentures and Government bonds would give the holders of them what they want— a really constant income. The ordinary shareholders in a public

---

[1] Sliding scales, admirable as is their general effect, perhaps err by being too simple. A sliding scale in the iron trade, for instance, should, I think, take account not only of the price of the finished iron, but also, on the one hand, of the prices of iron ore, coal, and other expenses of the employer, and, on the other, of the prices of the things chiefly consumed by the workmen. Trades in which sliding scales are possible could arrange special units for themselves, by aid of the statistics on which Government would base its general unit.

company would no longer be led to take an over-sanguine estimate of their position by a period of prosperity, which, besides enriching them directly, diminished the real payments which they have to make to debenture holders and perhaps to preference stock holders. And, on the other hand, they would not be oppressed by the extra weight of having to pay more than their real value on account of these fixed charges when prices were low and business drooping.

The standard unit of purchasing power being published, the Law Courts should, I think, give every facility to contracts, wills, and other documents made in terms of the unit; and Government itself might gradually feel its way towards assessing rates and taxes (except, of course, such things as payments for postage stamps) in terms of the unit, and also towards reckoning the salaries, pensions, and, when possible, the wages of its employees at so many units instead of so much currency. It should, I think, begin by offering, as soon as the unit was made, to pay for each £100 of Consols a really uniform interest of three units, instead of a nominally uniform but really fluctuating interest of £3. The public, though at first regarding the new notion as uncanny, would, I believe, take to it rapidly as soon as they got to see its substantial advantages. Their dislike of it even at first would be less than was their dislike of coal fires, of railways, and of gas. Ere long the currency would, I believe, be restricted to the functions for which it is well fitted, of measuring and settling transactions that are completed shortly after they are begun. I think we ought, without delay, to set about preparing for voluntary use an authoritative unit; being voluntary it would be introduced tentatively, and would be a powerful remedy for a great evil. This plan would not cause any forced disturbance of existing contracts, such as would result from a change of our currency. It would give a better standard for deferred payments than could possibly be given by a currency (as ordinarily understood), and therefore would diminish the temptation to hurry on impetuously a change of our currency with the object of making its value a little more stable; and it could be worked equally well with any currency. . . .

2. ENGLISH CLASSICAL POLITICAL ECONOMY
AND THE DEBATE ON INDEXATION

BRIAN GRIFFITHS

THE QUESTION of whether, and how, a country's legal standard of value should be adjusted to correct for the distortion created by rising or falling prices seems to have been discussed by 19th-century writers following periods of fairly substantial inflation and deflation. The Napoleonic Wars and the aftermath was a period of fairly rapid inflation followed by a rather sharp deflation; between 1792 and 1814 prices rose by just over 60 per cent, between 1814 and 1822 they fell by 40 per cent. At least three writers in the 1820s and 1830s, Joseph Lowe, G. Poulett Scrope and G. R. Porter, analysed the effects of inflation and proposed correcting the standard of value for changes in the cost of living. They set out to show that in the first place it was possible to construct an index of consumer prices. Lowe proposed that the prices of staple articles of household consumption should be collected regularly and that a 'table of reference' should be framed showing the weighting attached to various commodities. Although Porter produced a table showing the average monthly fluctuations of 50 leading commodities between 1833 and 1837, none of the three attempted to work out the details of how such an index might be constructed.

Joseph Lowe
Of the three studies, by far the best is Joseph Lowe's *The Present State of England in Regard to Agriculture, Trade and Finance, with a Comparison of the Prospects of England and France* (1822). Both the purpose and general outline of his scheme are very clear:

'a table exhibiting from year to year, the power of money in purchase would give to annuitants and other contracting parties, the means of maintaining an agreement, not in its letter only, but in its spirit; of conferring on a specified sum a uniformity and permanency of value, by *changing the numerical value in proportion of the change in its power of purchase*'.

Such an adjustment might be made every three, five or seven years.

Lowe was particularly perceptive in his analysis of the beneficial effects of such a scheme on agriculture, the labour market, and the national debt. Because of uncertainty about the value of money, landlords are reluctant to agree to long leases during periods of inflation while tenants are reluctant to accept such leases during periods of deflation. The effect is that rents tend to be fixed in terms of the price of corn or that the land is not leased at all. Both results are harmful. If, however, the money value of rent were to be corrected for inflation, the problems would not arise and agriculture would maintain its prosperity.

His description of the labour market seems remarkably prescient. He claimed that the previous 30 years had been a time of frequent contention between employer and employed, and that wages in the metropolis were sticky in a downward direction, with real wages being too high during the period of deflation.

'Wages, salaries, professional fees are almost all on as high a scale as during the war, notwithstanding the cessation of the two great causes of the rise—the expense of living and the extra demand for labour. The persons whether of high or low station, who are in receipt of the established allowance if called on for an abatement, would naturally plead the uncertainty of provisions continuing at their present rate; and nothing it is evident will induce them willingly to assent to a reduction, except a guarantee against a recurrence of the grand evil—a rise in prices. In this most desirable object we should hope to succeed, not by a compulsory course, not by an interference between the payer and the receiver, but by an alternative offered to their voluntary adoption by putting it in their power, when making a time contract, to give a permanent value to a money stipulation, or to find when no such precaution was taken, an equitable standard of reference.

'Such a regulator would carry conviction to all parties and operate greatly to abridge altercation. At a time like the present it would relieve the inferior from much of the anxiety and humiliation attendant on reduction; and in the case of a rise in prices it would guide the employer to a fairer advance of wages, the distributor of charitable aid to a fair apportionment of relief.'

Although he did not venture into details of how the value of government bonds would be adjusted for inflation, he seems to have suggested that the price of the stock would rise *pari passu* with the index of inflation, as would the income from bonds. Therefore, no matter 'whether the country was at peace or war; whether its currency were sound or depreciated; whether the mines of gold and silver throughout the world became more or less productive' we should be assured of 'a permanent value to our public dividends'.

As a precedent Lowe mentioned the Court of Teinds and the tithe of Scotland. The Court decided that clerical income should be regulated by the price of corn in the public market over a series of years.

In conclusion he asked why such a scheme had not been adopted. His answer was twofold:

'the unfortunate neglect of political economy in the education of our public men; and the interest of government, the greatest of all debtors, to allow money to undergo a gradual depreciation'.

W. Stanley Jevons

In his book *Money and the Mechanisms of Exchange* (1875), W. Stanley Jevons argued very forcefully for a better standard of value.

'The question thus arises whether the progress of economical and statistical science might not enable us to devise some better standard of value. We have seen (pp. 136–143) that the so-called double standard system of money spreads the fluctuations of supply and demand of gold and silver over a larger area, and maintains both metals more unchanged in value than they would otherwise be. Can we not conceive a multiple legal tender, which would be still less liable to variation? We estimate the value of one hundred pounds by the quantities of corn, beef, potatoes, coal, timber, iron, tea, coffee, beer, and other principal commodities, which it will purchase from time to time. Might we not invent a legal tender note which should be convertible, not into any one single commodity, but into an aggregate of small quantities of various commodities, the quantity and quality of each being rigorously defined? Thus a hundred pound note would give the owners a right to demand one quarter of good wheat, one ton of ordinary merchant bar iron, one hundred pounds weight of middling cotton, twenty pounds of sugar, five pounds of tea, and other articles sufficient to make up the value. All these commodities will, of course, fluctuate in their relative values, but if the holder of the note loses upon some, he will in all probability gain upon others, so that on the average his note will remain steady in purchasing power. Indeed, as the articles into which it is convertible are those needed for continual consumption, the purchasing power of the note must remain steady compared with that of gold or silver, which metals are employed only for a few special purposes.'

Although such a currency would be impracticable, because no one wished to have all the articles included in the standard, he proposed the creation of a 'tabular standard of value', changes of which would be used to adjust the value of contracts fixed in money terms. He suggested that, to implement such a proposal, a permanent government commission would have to be created and endowed with a kind of judicial power. The officers of the commission would collect current commodity prices 'in all the principal markets of the kingdom' and then compute the average variations in the purchasing power of gold. The decisions of the commission would be published monthly and payments for wages, rents, annuities, etc. would be adjusted in accordance with them; at first the scheme would be entirely voluntary, but then after its undoubted value had been shown it would be made compulsory for every debt over three months.

The scheme Jevons suggested had many advantages: it would result in a whole new degree of stability in social relations; it would guarantee the fixed incomes of individuals and public institutions; speculation would be discouraged; the calculations of merchants would be less frequently frustrated by causes beyond their own control; and many bankruptcies would be averted, as the intensity of crises was lessened, because as prices fell, the liabilities of debtors would decrease proportionately. The only real difficulty Jevons saw with such a scheme was the method by which changes in the purchasing power of gold were to be calculated.

Walter Bagehot

Bagehot thought differently. In an article in the *Economist* (20 November, 1875), he raised four objections to Jevons's proposal. First, it would be wholly unfit for a country with foreign trade. It would discourage trade because of the increased uncertainty in exchanging currency for gold. London had developed as a financial centre because of the stability of its standard and this was one way to wreck it. Secondly, it would make banking impossible, as a banker would never know what he owed; each debt, being contracted at a different time, would have an uncertain value. Thirdly, Bagehot foresaw severe difficulties in calculating the index, especially in maintaining a constant quality for the articles included. Lastly, in a good currency the paying medium ought either to be identical with, or readily interchangeable into, a definite quantity of the standard of value. But in the Jevons proposal, the standard was fixed while the paying medium was in a state of incessant fluctuation. For these reasons Bagehot felt that 'we must adhere to one or other of the precious metals as a standard of value, like our forefathers'.

Robert Giffen

In an article in the *Economic Journal* for 1892 entitled 'Fancy Monetary Standard', which is a reply to an article in the previous issue by Mr Aneurin Williams entitled 'A Value of Bullion Standard' (a proposal to provide for an issue of paper which was to consist of promises to pay a varying quality of bullion, the variation depending on the change in a specified index number), Robert Giffen restated Bagehot's objections concluding that they were 'altogether so destructive as to make it unnecessary to go farther', but nevertheless added some of his own. Firstly, he argued that monetary standards should not be changed unless the reasons were overwhelming. Because good money was so very difficult to get and most governments, when they meddled with money, were apt to make great blunders, the standard for money was best left alone. Secondly, he claimed that the proposal would only be feasible with an inconvertible and managed paper. Thirdly, there was the problem of actually constructing the index. Lastly, the problem of adjusting wages over short periods to changes in the index would give rise to difficulties in the labour market.

Alfred Marshall

Alfred Marshall's proposals for establishing a unit of constant general purchasing power were set out in a paper read at the 'Industrial Remuneration Conference' in 1885, which was subsequently included in his answers to questions put by the Royal Commission on The Depression of Trade and Industry (1886) and in an article published in the *Contemporary Review* for March 1887, which was included in a memorandum submitted by him to the Royal Commission on the Values of Gold and Silver (1887, 1888), parts of which are reproduced elsewhere in these Notes.[1] Unlike that of Jevons's multiple legal standard, the essence of his plan was not to change the form of the currency but to adjust the value of all contracts fixed in money terms for changes in the average price level. He also put forward a proposal for changing the form of the currency so as to make it a true bimetallic standard, but he was very careful to separate the two schemes, and also to warn against the possible dangers of changing the base of the currency.

In an exchange of letters with Professor Irving Fisher in 1911 and 1912, Marshall remained convinced of the value of the proposals which he put forward 25 years earlier.

'But a quarter of a century has made me ever more desirous that every country should have an official "unit" of general purchasing power, made up from tables of price percentages like those of Sauerbeck and others: and that it should authorise long-period obligations for the payment of rent and interest on loans of all kinds to be made at the option of the

---

[1] Above, pp. 33–38.

contracting parties, in terms either of this general unit, or of a selection of price percentages appropriate to the special purpose in hand. Public authority should make out such lists as appeared suitable to particular classes of transactions: but the parties concerned should have perfect freedom to make special selections. Any wages contract, such as a sliding scale in the iron trade, might "take account not only of the price of the finished iron, but also on the one hand, of the prices of iron ore, coal, and other expenses of the employer; and on the other, of the price of the things chiefly consumed by the workmen".

'I think that could be done at once. If it succeeded, the world would, I think, be prepared in say twenty years for an international "fixed standard" paper currency, provided that it can be helped on the way by a vigorous movement such as that in which you are active.' (dated 16-IX-1911).

In a third letter to Fisher dated 15-X-1912, he throws some light on Giffen's earlier article and his own doubts about the scheme.

'When Giffen uttered his vehement trumpet blast against "Fancy Monetary Standards" I chaffed him about his energy, and I recollect that he said that his argument was not opposed to my scheme. Recollecting that just now, I further remember that my doubt about the practicability of my original scheme was connected with International Stock Exchange Securities bearing a fixed rate of interest (among other things).'

J. M. Keynes

Recalling Marshall's proposals of the 1880s, J. M. Keynes, one of Marshall's great admirers, recommended to the Royal Commission on National Debt and Taxation (1927) in 1924 that the government should issue an index-linked bond, claiming that the advantages of such a scheme were even greater than in the 1880s.

'I suggest that there is one further type of bond not yet in issue which might prove popular with particular individuals and so enable the State to raise funds a little more cheaply. I suggest that there should be issued bonds of which the capital and the interest would be paid not in a fixed amount of sterling, but in such amount of sterling as has a fixed commodity value as indicated by an index number. I think that an official index number should be established for such purposes on the lines of the optional tabular standard recommended long ago by Dr Marshall, and that it should be open to anyone, including particularly the Treasury, to offer loans, the payment of the interest on which and the repayment of the capital of which would be governed by movements of the index number. I can say from knowledge that there are many investors, who, wishing to take no risks would naturally confine themselves to trustee stocks, yet feel a natural anxiety in being compelled to invest their whole resources in terms of legal tender money, the relation of which to real value has been shown by experience to be variable. Throughout almost the whole of

Europe investors of the trustee type have been deprived in the past ten years of the greater part of the value of their property. Even here in England all such investors have suffered a very large real loss. We may hope that great instability in the value of the currency may not be one of the things which the future has in store for us. But it is natural that some people should be anxious about it. Unless, therefore, the Treasury hopes to make a profit through the depreciation of legal tender, it would lose nothing, and might gain something in terms of interest, by issuing such bonds as I have indicated.'

Otto Niemeyer

The Commission raised the practicability of such a proposal with Sir Otto E. Niemeyer, Controller of Finance at the Treasury. His opinion of the scheme was that he did 'not quite see why it should attract anybody' and that although some investors did take such a 'long and elaborate view', for ordinary people 'this would be too clever altogether'. For Sir Otto such a proposal was connected with countries which had experienced great changes in the value of money such as Germany, which was not the expectation of the UK. In any case, when the Treasury had issued 5- to 15-year bonds, the interest on which varied according to Treasury Bill rate, which he claimed was similar to Keynes's proposal, they were not a success. He was of the opinion that before the state issued such a bond he would like to see it tried in practice by a private person, such as one of the more enterprising insurance companies.

3. INDEXATION: A BIBLIOGRAPHY

I. EARLY CONTROVERSY

Lowe, Joseph, *The Present State of England in regard to Agriculture, Trade, and Finance, with a comparison of the prospects of England and France*, London, 1822.

Scrope, G. Poulett, *An Examination of the Bank Charter Question with an Inquiry into the Nature of a Just Standard of Value*, London, 1833.

Porter, G. R., *Principles of Political Economy*, London, 1833.
— *Political Economy for Plain People*, London, 1833.
— *The Progress of the Nation*, London, 1838.

Jevons, W. S. (1875): 'A Tabular Standard of Value', Chapter XXV of *Money and the Mechanism of Exchange*, New York, 1898, pp. 318–26.

Bagehot, Walter (1875): 'A New Standard of Value', *Economist*, London, 20 November, 1875; reprinted in *Economic Journal*, London, Vol. II, 1892, pp. 472–77.

Giffen, R. (1892): 'Fancy Monetary Standards', *Economic Journal*, London, Vol. II, 1892, pp. 463–71.

Marshall, Alfred (1886): Reply to the Royal Commission on the Depression of Trade and Industry, reproduced in *Official Papers by Alfred Marshall*, Macmillan, London, 1926, pp. 9–12.
— (1887): article in *Contemporary Review*, March 1887, reproduced in *Memorials of Alfred Marshall*, ed. A. C. Pigou, Macmillan, London, 1925, pp. 188–211.
— (1911): letter to Irving Fisher, reproduced in *Memorials of Alfred Marshall*, p. 476.

Keynes, J. M. (1927): Evidence Presented to the Committee on National Debt and Taxation, in *Minutes of Evidence* (Colwyn Committee), HMSO, London, 1927, Vol. I, p. 278 and p. 287.

Niemeyer, Sir Otto (1927): dismissal of Keynes's proposal (as above), *Minutes of Evidence*, Vol. II, p. 633.

'Agenda for the Age of Inflation—II', *Economist*, 25 August, 1951, pp. 435–37.

II. Official Reports

United Kingdom

Committee on the Working of the Monetary System (Radcliffe Committee, August 1959):
  Report, Cmnd. 827, HMSO, London, 1959, pp. 211–2.
  Memoranda of Evidence, Vol. 3, part XIII, no. 6, pp. 66–9.
  Minutes of Evidence, qq. 10,043–141, pp. 663–4.

Committee to Review National Savings (Page Committee, June 1973):
  Report, Cmnd. 5273, HMSO, London, pp. 190–8, 309–14.

United States

Joint Committee on the Economic Report, *Monetary Policy and the Management of the Public Debt*, 82nd Congress, 2nd Session, Washington, 1952:
  Friedman, Milton, and Machlup, Fritz, before the Patman Subcommittee: pp. 1,105–6.
  Replies of Treasury and Council of Economic Advisers: pp. 142–5, pp. 888–9.

Commission on Money and Credit, *Fiscal and Debt Management Policies*, pp. 202–13:
  Tobin, James, 'An essay on principles of debt management' (Englewood Cliffs, N.J., 1963).

Commission on Money and Credit, *Inflation, Growth and Employment*, pp. 177–229:
  Holzman, F. D., 'Escalation and its Use to Mitigate the Inequities of Inflation' (Englewood Cliffs, N.J., 1964).

II. International Agencies

Finch, David, 'Purchasing Power Guarantees for Deferred Payments', *IMF Staff Papers*, February 1956, pp. 1–22.

OECD, Committee for Invisible Transactions, Capital Markets Study Vol. II, *Formation of Savings*, Paris, 1968, pp. 39–41, 97–105, 139–140, 176, 194.

Lall, S., 'Countering Inflation: the Role of Value Linking', *Finance and Development*, June 1969, pp. 10–15.

Liefmann-Keil, Elizabeth, 'Index-based Adjustments for Social Security Benefits', *International Labour Review*, May 1959, pp. 487–510.

OECD, Committee on Financial Markets, *Indexation of Fixed-Interest Securities*, Paris, 1974.

UN, *Economic Bulletin for Latin America*, 'Index Clauses in Deferred Payments', October 1957, pp. 73–89.

IV. ACADEMIC PAPERS

Hein, J., 'A note on the use of index clauses abroad', *Journal of Finance*, No. 15, December 1960, pp. 546–52.

Arvidsson, G., 'Should we have indexed loans?', in D. C. Hague (ed.), *Inflation*, New York, 1962, pp. 112–126.
'Reflections on Index Loans', *Skandinaviska Banken Quarterly Review*, 40–41, 1959–60, pp. 1–14.

Morag, Amotz, 'For an Inflation-proof Economy', *American Economic Review*, March 1962, pp. 177–85.

Eagly, Robert, 'An Interpretation of Palander's Twin Securities Markets Proposal', *Southern Economic Journal*, July 1960, pp. 51–4.
'On Government Issuance of an Index Bond', *Public Finance*, 1967, no. 3, pp. 268–84.

Bach, G. L., and Musgrave, R. A., 'A Stable Purchasing Power Bond', *American Economic Review*, December 1941, pp. 823–5.

Cohen, B. I., 'The use of indexed debts in underdeveloped countries', *Public Finance*, 1966, No. 4, pp. 441–457.

Goode, Richard, 'A Constant Purchasing-Power Savings Bond', *National Tax Journal*, IV, 1951, pp. 332–40.

Sarnat, Marshall, 'Purchasing Power Risk, Portfolio Analysis, and the Case for Index-Linked Bonds', *Journal of Money, Credit and Banking*, August 1973, pp. 836–45.

Robson, Peter, 'Index-Linked Bonds', *Review of Economic Studies* No. 75, October 1960, pp. 57–68.
'Inflation-Proof Loans', *National Westminster Bank Quarterly Review*, May 1974, pp. 48–60.

[48]

4. FISCAL DRAG AND INFLATION

'Higher Taxation without representation' in Britain

THE PHENOMENON 'fiscal drag' to which Professor Friedman draws attention in the USA,[1] is just as evident in the UK. As money incomes rise—even though this may be no more than enough to keep pace with rising prices—people move into higher tax brackets and their average rate of tax automatically increases.

Table 1 shows that although the standard rate of income tax on earned income (after allowing for earned income relief) fell from 36 per cent in 1949–50 and 38 per cent in 1951–52 to 30 per cent in 1973–74, income tax as a proportion of total personal income rose

TABLE 1

UK Income Tax: 1949–50 to 1973–74

	Standard rate of tax on earned income[1]	Initial range of income at nil or reduced tax rate[2]	Income tax as proportion of total personal income[3]
	%	£ p.a.	%
1949–50	36	550	9.5
1951–52	38	580	9.6
1969–70	32	865	13.2
1973–74	30	1,175	12.7

[1] After allowing for earned income relief at full rate. (From 1973–74 the 'basic' rate is for earned income and earned income relief has been abolished.)

[2] Personal allowances plus reduced tax band (up to 1969–70) for a married couple with two children aged not over 11.

[3] From National Income data. The total of personal incomes includes items which are not strictly 'personal' (e.g. income of sole traders and partnerships). Alternative data, from Inland Revenue income surveys, give a similar result. From 1949–50 to 1969–70 income tax as a proportion of personal income (on their definition) rose from 13 per cent to 17 per cent. (Inland Revenue, *Survey of Personal Incomes 1969–70*, HMSO, p. 3.)

from about 10 per cent to about 13 per cent. Also during the postwar period the initial amount of income which was either exempt from tax or charged at less than standard rate, for a married couple with two children aged up to 11 years, increased from £550 to £1,175. As in the USA, therefore, the proportion of income paid in income tax rose in spite of *reductions* in tax rates and increases in initial

[1] 'Inflation—Proofing the Income Tax', *Newsweek*, 13 May, 1974.

allowances. The relief served to moderate, but not eliminate, the rise in effective average tax rate due to rising money incomes.

The amount of income tax paid rose from £1,007 million in 1949 to £7,803 million in 1973 (7.7 times) while personal income rose from £10,571 million to £61,583 million (5.8 times).

Table 2 shows, for a family with two children aged up to 11, the average rate of income tax paid on various incomes at 1974–75 tax rates, and the rate that would be paid in 1984 if incomes had doubled to keep pace with inflation (i.e. assuming, as Professor Friedman did, an inflation rate of 7 per cent per annum). The figures show that with *no* increase in real income and *no* change in tax rates for a given money income, the effective rate of tax would nevertheless increase substantially. The proportionate rise in tax rate would be most severe for people with lower incomes (multiplied about four times for a family with £1,500 income in 1974 rising to £3,000 in 1984, compared with about one-and-a-half times for a family with £10,000 income in 1974 rising to £20,000 in 1984).

The reason for the more severe effect for people with lower incomes

TABLE 2

Actual Income Tax Rate in 1974
and Tax Rate in 1984 if Income Doubles (UK)

Married couple with two children aged up to 11

Income before tax: 1974	Income tax as % of Income:	
	1974 actual	1984 (income doubled)
£ p.a.	%	%
1,500	5	19
2,000	12	22
2,500	16	25
3,000	19	26
4,000	22	31
5,000	25	35
10,000	35	51

Note: Tax rates are for 1974–75 (Budget proposals of March 1974). The basic rate was raised from 30 per cent to 33 per cent and all higher rates also increased by 3 per cent (except the top rate on income over £20,000 which was raised by 8 per cent to 83 per cent). All income is assumed to be earned. In assessing tax it is assumed that family allowance is claimed and the tax includes 'claw-back'.

is that the tax rate on additional income (marginal rate) has a much higher ratio to the existing average rate, which is low because of the effect of the personal allowances. Thus for the family with £1,500 income the existing average rate of tax is only 4.6 per cent (shown as 5 per cent in Table 2). The marginal rate of tax on the next £1,500 is 33 per cent (the new 'basic' rate of tax in 1974–75), so that the marginal rate is about seven times the existing average rate. For the family with £10,000 income the existing average rate of tax is 35 per cent and the marginal rate on the next £10,000 is about 69 per cent, so that the marginal rate is only about double the existing average rate.

Inflation favours the rich

In practice, the effect of 'fiscal drag' in the UK during the post-war years has been (as pointed out in the IEA study, *How Much In-equality?*)[1] to counteract the trend towards equality of incomes before tax. After tax, the trend has been less marked. The reduction in the standard rate of income tax has resulted in a reduced proportion of income levied in tax among the highest 1 per cent of incomes, while lower down the scale rising incomes have led to an automatic increase in the effective rate of tax. Professor Friedman's proposal for automatic adjustment of tax allowances and the limits of tax brackets to allow for inflation would (among its other advantages) remove the tendency for the existing tax system to bring about unintended redistribution in favour of the better-off.

[1] Research Monograph 31, 1974.

Statistics on British Inflation

TABLE 1
Retail Prices: UK, 1963 to 1974

	Index: 1970 = 100	Annual increase %
1963	73.8	
1964	76.7	3.9
1965	80.2	4.6
1966	83.2	3.7
1967	85.2	2.4
1968	89.3	4.8
1969	93.9	5.2
1970	100.0	6.5
1971	109.5	9.5
1972	117.0	6.8
1973	126.8	8.4
	___	___
1974 (1st Quarter)	137.2	12.3[1]

[1] 1st Quarter compared with 1st Quarter 1973 (122.2).
Source: Based on official statistics (Department of Employment).

TABLE 2
Prices of Materials Used in Manufacturing: UK, 1963 to 1974

	Index: 1970 = 100	Annual % increase or decrease (—)
1963	79.2	
1964	82.5	4.2
1965	83.5	1.2
1966	85.6	2.5
1967	85.2	—0.5
1968	92.9	9.0
1969	95.0	2.3
1970	100.0	5.3
1971	104.6	4.6
1972	109.2	4.4
1973	144.3	32.1
	___	___
1974 (1st Quarter)	206.5	63.9[1]

[1] 1st Quarter compared with 1st Quarter 1973 (126.0).
Source: Based on official statistics (Department of Trade and Industry).

TABLE 3

Weekly Earnings (All Industries): UK, 1963 to 1973

	Index: 1970 = 100	Annual increase %
1963	60.8	
1964	65.1	7.1
1965	70.0	7.5
1966	74.5	6.4
1967	77.0	3.4
1968	83.2	8.1
1969	89.7	7.8
1970	100.0	11.5
1971	111.2	11.2
1972	125.1	12.5
1973	142.4	13.8

Source: Based on official statistics (Department of Employment).

TABLE 4

Money Supply: UK, 1963 to 1973

	Money Stock (M_3) at end of year £ million	Annual increase[2] %
1963	11,516	
1964	12,155	5.7
1965	13,083	7.7
1966	13,555	3.7
1967	15,003[1]	9.9
1968	16,092	7.7
1969	16,596	3.1
1970	18,175	9.6
1971	20,541	13.0
1972	26,245	25.8
1973	33,431	27.5

[1] £14,895 million before including institutions newly classified as banks in 1967.
[2] Based on increase during the year, excluding effects of changes in definition of banks and allowance for hoarding, etc., in annual levels of coin in circulation.

Note: Money Stock (M_3) includes currency in circulation and all resident deposits with banks and discount houses.

Source: Central Statistical Office.

TABLE 5

Value per Unit of Imports and Exports: UK, 1965 to 1973

| | Imports | | Exports | |
	Index of Unit Value 1970 = 100	Annual Increase %	Index of Unit Value 1970 = 100	Annual Increase %
1965	81		79	
1966	83	2.5	82	3.8
1967	83	—	83	1.2
1968	93	12.0	90	8.4
1969	96	3.2	93	3.3
1970	100	4.2	100	7.5
1971	104	4.0	106	6.0
1972	109	4.8	111	4.7
1973	140	28.4	125	12.6

Source: Based on official statistics: balance-of-payments basis (Department of Trade and Industry).

TABLE 6

Price Increase in UK and Other Countries, 1970 to 1973

	Increase in consumer prices 1970–73 %
UK	26.8
Netherlands	25.2
Japan	23.9
Italy	22.8
France	19.9
Germany	18.8
Canada	16.0
USA	14.4

Source: Based on official statistics (OECD, etc.).

FRIEDMAN'S MAIN WRITINGS FOR THE IEA

Occasional Paper 33
The Counter-Revolution in Monetary Theory
Fourth Impression 1978   50p
'It was a brilliant exposition of the theory which he has done so much
to develop. In practical terms his message was one whose relevance
was immediately apparent to his audience. You can only contain
inflation, the argument ran, if you control the money supply.'
Director

Occasional Paper 41
Monetary Correction
Third Impression 1978   £1.00
'. . . devoted to setting out, with typical verve and vigour, a case for
indexation based on a mixture of arguments from justice and from
expediency. Both categories are extremely interesting and thought
provoking . . .'
A. B. Cramp, *Economic Journal*

Occasional Paper 44
Unemployment versus Inflation?
Third Impression 1977   £1.00
'. . . what is perhaps the most important economic pamphlet to be
published in the UK for several decades.'
Samuel Brittan, *Financial Times*

Occasional Paper 49
From Galbraith to Economic Freedom
Second Impression 1977   £1.00
Those who learn their economics from the extravagant BBC series
involving Professor Galbraith may end up with some odd concepts
of the world of industry and commerce. Those who are impressed by
the series should read as an antidote "From Galbraith to Economic
Freedom".'
Leader, *Yorkshire Post*

Occasional Paper 51
Inflation and Unemployment: The New Dimension of Politics
Second Impression 1978   £1.00
'I have to warn you that there is neither shock nor horror nor sen-
sation in his lecture, only close reasoning, and a sense of scholarly
inquiry . . . I urge readers to buy and read the lecture.'
Patrick Hutber, *Sunday Telegraph*

[55]

IEA OCCASIONAL PAPERS in print

FRIEDMAN. Monetary correction.

<u>copy A</u>